Please Return
~~Mary Ellen Lazareck~~
~~736-6745~~
~~286 Clinton St, Whitesboro, NY~~
13492

THE
MOMENT
OF THE
N<u>OW</u>!

Sharon LaBella
735-7946

THE MOMENT OF THE NOW

by
Nina-Marie

Nina-Marie Publications
Elk Grove Village, Illinois

Unless otherwise indicated, Scripture quotations are taken from the following translations of the Holy Bible:

The Holy Bible, King James Version, Scofield Reference Bible. Copyright renewed 1937, 1945 Oxford University Press. New York.

The Holy Bible, New International Version. Copyright 1973, 1978, 1984 International Bible Society. Grand Rapids, Michigan.

Ryrie Study Bible, Expanded Edition, King James Version. Copyright 1986, 1994 Moody Bible Institute of Chicago. Chicago, Illinois.

The New Open Bible, Study Edition. Copyright 1990, 1985, 1983 Thomas Nelson, Inc. Memphis, Tennessee.

You must reach a place in your walk with God, where you realize the past is in another place, the future a promise until manifested as real, and you stand solely in your today as it unfolds
..... moment .....by moment ..... by moment

Nina-Marie Leslie

DEDICATED TO:

The Father, the Son, and the Holy Spirit for the roles that each of You play in my life. Thank You Father for Your covering, thank You Lord Jesus for Your loving, and thank You Holy Spirit for Your teaching. I love You all forever!

My husband, the late Senior Pastor Donn M. Leslie, for loving me, supporting me, believing in me, and entrusting me with his vision. If I am a missile, and I am, you will always be my launching pad. You told me I would write but you didn't tell me it would be without you.

My mother and first mentor, Dr. Mom (Dorothy Carter-Lindsey) for your unfailing love. You were right. The acorn doesn't fall too far from the tree! Love you first.

My sisters, Robin Elaine Tate and Dr. Allison Lindsey-Dixon for their strong love, nerve-racking honesty, and keen discernment. Without a solid foundation the strongest column falls. You are my rocks and I thank you both for always being there. You take such good care of me. Love you first because I was here first!

My second mentor, Dr. Richard D. Henton of Monument of Faith in Chicago, IL. You believed in me when I didn't believe in myself. Behold the fulfillment of the Word of the Lord from your mouth that you spoke the night you preached "God's Chosen Children of Destiny." Everyone on the earth needs this word! I love you, Poppa.

To Oasis Church International: You know you know how to love somebody! I am honored to lead you forward. Let us build on what our "Bishop" started and "run on to see what the end will be!" I love each of your little "roundhead" selves. Now let's go on from this place.

To the Oasis Covenant Churches for truly cutting covenant and manifesting love:

Word of Truth International Christian Center
Pastor Michael Brown
Pastor Pamela Brown

New Beginnings International Christian Ministries
Senior Pastor Larry E. Avant
Pastor Catherine Avant

CONTENTS

AUTHOR'S NOTE

Beloved of God,

This book has disturbed my sleep and occupied my thoughts for the last nine years. I have tried to publish it twice before but my efforts were to no avail. This is the right time. This is the moment for which this book was born.

As a writer, minister, or educator, you always live what you preach or teach because you experience it first hand. Simply put, when Father God gives you a stick (a word) it always hits you first. I have been prophetically and apostolically throttled and challenged with this revelation in my personal life. I know it will be applicable to your life because it has been applicable to mine.

I know that this writing is coming forth in the moment of the now. I have earnestly sought the Lord for clarity regarding time. What He has shared with me, I hope and pray will be a strength and a blessing to your life.

You have options. Do or die. Obey or disobey. Surrender or control. Lead or be led. The choices are yours to make. Hear ye the Word of the Lord! The choices and the decisions that you make in this season will affect the next 12-15 years of your life. You cannot afford to hit or miss. You must inquire of the Lord, hear Him clearly, and move to immediately obey Him. Obey as fast as you can.

The Father has a blueprint and a master plan mapped out for your life. It is called your destiny. His plans are going to blow your mind in the days to come. Heaven has booked your calendar and it is full of destiny! Destiny equals work, not fantasy. You must roll up your sleeves, prepare to work hard, and apply yourself to your destiny.

It is my heart's cry that this writing will bring clarity to some unclear areas, water to some dry places, and healing to all of the toxic places in your life. Know that you are not alone on this journey. Jesus promised that He would be with us always, even unto the end. I believe Him and take Him at His Word. Will you?

Get into the now of God and leave yesterday behind. The moment of the now is your address in the Spirit. Your obedience will determine your zip code. Stay where God places you and know that He is there with you. He is a very present help and His help is perpetually present. Be blessed in Christ Jesus!

Nina-Marie Leslie

PERSONAL PRAYER

Father, in the Name of Jesus,

We thank You for all that You have done for us. We acknowledge Your presence in the creative processes of our lives. We honor You for Your lovingkindness and for Your tender mercies. We say great is Thy faithfulness. We thank You for Your patience and the many roles You play in our lives.

We now release You to go into the moments of our yesterdays and bury every dead thing, every indiscretion, every failure, every missed opportunity, and every time we missed You. We now bury our personal condemnation and let it go. We acknowledge it now and let it die.

We say that You alone are the God of the Moment. You alone are the eternal God and Creator. You are our Creator and we give You total rule and reign to create in us severally as You will. We release You to do in us, as You so desire. We give You praise, honor, and all glory because You are worthy to be praised.

We thank You for the moving of Your Spirit. We choose to let go of every hurt, every hindrance, and every failure. We receive Your comfort. Lord Jesus, we now receive an understanding of Your times. We say that our times are in Your hands and You alone have the master plan.

We receive the new life of Your spirit flowing to the inside of us. We celebrate every opportunity that You are placing in us, on us, and around us. We give You high praise as we walk into the moment of the now. Feed us and we will be well fed of Thee. Wash us and we will be cleansed by Thy hands. Thank You, Lord Jesus.

(Now you give God some praise!)

1

MY HEART'S CRY

As I child, I was always interested in concepts of time. I remember wanting a "big girl" watch. When we opened Christmas gifts, my sisters and girl cousins would scream for Barbie watches, but I wanted a big shiny Timex and Bobsey Twin books. Even as a young girl, I would ask my grandfather about God and heaven and the clocks up there. He would gently shush me and say I was too little to care or know about time in heaven.

In hindsight I realize my verbal command was not developed enough to communicate my questions and the thought processes of my heart. That is why it is so important to take the time to hear the questions of a child's heart. I now know that I was inquiring about a great portion of my of destiny and did not know it then.

In 1989, the Spirit of the Lord began dealing with me regarding the word, "time." Whether it was the vastness of time, seasons of time, dimensions of time, or something akin, it blew my mind to process that at all times ever, He has been. In all times, He is and in all times, He shall be because time is born, birthed, and established of Him.

When I talked with people in Christian circles, the schools of thought regarding time were vague. The Christians who I dialogued with did not want to discuss or ponder the meanings of time. One church leader told me, "Nina girl, you always thinking so deep! You want to know too much. You just gotta trust God like everybody else! You ain't Plato and you ain't Socrates! God don't have to give you no answers. He's God all by Himself and He don't need nobody's help."

So I submitted to that leader and left the cognitive part of myself alone. . .for about 15 minutes. Then there was this little persistent niggling in my spirit that would not let up. I kept hearing, "I cause you to think. I cause you to think." Not being filled with the Holy Spirit then, I thought that was my "head-voice." The same one that would tell me, "Don't let that boy kiss you, be a good girl." I kept hearing the questions, other questions, and then more questions.

My eternal search for truth would often annoy my elders and get me sent to my room This allotted me more time to sit and think. As a child, the Holy Spirit was expanding my conscious mind to accommodate the destiny He had planned for my life in Christ Jesus.

When I talked with friends who were of alternate belief systems, they were intrigued with time and sought a greater understanding of it. It seemed that the Saints of God in my lifespace at that time would not and did not discourse about time and its relativity to kingdom living.

Those who practiced other worldly belief systems such as the mystic believers, psychic friends, and transactional analysis associates in my life were all willing to ponder concepts of time and its absorption in the universe. They were in awe of creation and its formal beginning. We spent hours defining our understanding of God and time. Even associates who were of alternate sexual expressions would sit and talk about time and where they believed life ended. The Saints during that season of my life were too busy shouting.

I believe in shouting but I also believe in thinking. God

has given us wonderful minds to process information. Many people hide behind, "You can't understand God. His ways are not your ways." I'm not trying to understand God. I'm endeavoring to totally obey Him. To obey someone's orders, you must get an understanding. In Proverbs 4:7 the Bible encourages us,

Wisdom is the principal thing; therefore get wisdom: and with all thy getting, get understanding.

I speak in tongues fluently. I prophesy in accuracy, brevity, and validity. I interpret dreams and have open eye visions. I believe in, embrace, and practice every mode of spirituality that Father God has given us. I endeavor with everything in me to be led by the Spirit of God. I walk in trust, I walk in sensitivity, and I feel God. I do thank God for cognition, intelligence, and a mind.

I also thank Him for feelings because in the same moment, I firmly believe God created us as cognitive creations. He ordained that we would be "thinking creations," not animals or autotrons. That is why salvation is a choice. That is why heaven is a choice. We are human and not animal. We cognitively walk by faith and not by sight (2 Corinthians 5:7). We decide to serve God (Zephaniah 3:9). We decide to live holy lives. It is a mandate but we must decide to live it (Leviticus 20:7). We decide who we will live for (Joshua 24:14).

Many times, things do not happen simply because God wants them to happen. After divinity speaks, there has to be a human decision to obey. 2 Peter 3:9 tells us that He is not willing that any should perish, but that all should come to repentance. It is His will and heart's desire that all would have eternal life. However, some will not because that is not their personal decision.

This is one of the many importances of prophetic ministry. Some people think just because they receive a prophetic word, it will automatically happen. That is not so. Sometimes the Word of the Lord is conditional, sometimes it is unconditional. It can be directional, revelational, confirmational, or instructional. It could be an encouragement or a word of comfort. The Word of the Lord requires a response. When a prophetic word comes, it generally brings "work" along with it. If the Word of the Lord comes saying you will receive a certain educational scholarship, it means you will go home and study to show yourself approved unto God. You will walk in discipline and not watch television all night. You will study and learn your lessons. Then, when the names are tossed in the pot, your name will be included because you fulfilled the laws of the earth to be considered. You can then rejoice as the Finance Committee reaches in to pull out the recipient's name. The Word of the Lord will cause your name to rise as cream to the top, and you'll receive the fulfillment of the spoken Word. But in order for your name to be pulled, it had to be in there.

It is time for you to make some decisions. You have put it off as long as possible. The moment is here. It is now time to bring your life into agreement with some decisions you've already made. You made the decisions before, you just never acted on them but the time is now. It's the right time and the timely time.

When I lived in Tulsa, one February required me to be out in itinerant ministry for 33 straight days. I used that time to really seek the Lord. I had come to an end of myself and could go not a step further. Do you know what it's like to honestly get to an end of who you are? I remember telling God, "I can hear You for everybody and his mama. Now I need to hear from You for myself." And He began to speak to me.

God used several scenes from the movie *Karate Kid* to minister to me and bring healing to my damaged heart. There is a part in the first portion when the bad guys are chasing the

Karate Kid with the explicit purpose of jacking him up. They had taunted and tortured him for a season. At the school party, he was able to get them back by throwing water on them. He was running and they were after him.

I was in the hotel sleeping when the Spirit of the Lord awakened me. He said, "Look at this" and just as I really focused in, they caught him. The Lord spoke to me again and said, "Look at this. I am going to heal you."

The kid was running and quickly scaling a fence. I felt like that was me, trying to run from the enemies of my life who were close on my heels. Just as he was scaling that fence, I felt like, "Thank God! Whew, he got away." Then the hand of the enemy reached out and grabbed his ankle. Something in me began to break up.

They pulled him down from the top and two of them held him up on each side. They began to do karate kicks to his rib cage and they began to beat him. The head guy kicked him in the face and they did all of the things you do in karate. And right when the head guy was extending his leg to deliver the death blow, if you looked at the enemy, you missed the help coming.

The primary focus is on the death blow about to be delivered. The secondary focus is on the help quietly coming up over the fence. Over the fence comes his mentor, Mr. Miaggi. Look out, devil. Here comes backup! You have backup in the Holy Ghost.

I was sitting there and I was crying so hard. I didn't have any tissue handy because I didn't know I was going to cry. So I picked up that bed pillow and sobbed into the pillow because I didn't want people to hear me through the walls.

Mr. Miaggi stood in the gap and truly made up the hedge. He kicked backside like it was going out of style. He didn't exert any extra energy. When he moved, he moved in purpose, he moved for a purpose, and he moved on purpose. Nothing was wasted or misdirected.

What really blessed me was after he finished fighting and being an avenger, (remember Jesus said, "It is finished") as soon as he turned away from the scene, he turned to express another facet of himself. He was instantly paternal. How like the heart of God. God would wipe out the armies of Israel's enemies but He was gentle with His tender little sheep. Jesus ascended and ever lives to make intercession for us, but He is also our friend in the time of trouble.

As he knelt over the inert figure of Daniel-Son, I thought, "Father, that's exactly how I feel. That's exactly where I am. I have taken all I can and I feel like Daniel-Son. I feel whipped, sore, and defeated." Then Miaggi knelt over the Kid and made two moves that began my healing process.

You need to see the movie and watch it prophetically to see the symbolism of how Miaggi scooped his arm under the Kid's neck and then gently but with great strength lifted the rest of him. The movements are gentle, yet fierce and protective. The Father showed me the importance of how Miaggi gently supported the neck first. The neck is so fragile and yet is the very strength of the spine. Had the Kid's rib been broken, it could have punctured the heart. As Miaggi laced his arms around the Kid's body, I felt the hands of God go around my body.

The Lord said, "Why won't you tell me what's going on with you? Why don't you talk to me?" I said, "I do." He said, "You praise me and tell me the regular things in your life. You ask me to cover you with my Blood. You give me praise through mess and act appropriately." He said, "You are a prophet of protocol and you know order but I am requiring nakedness. Tell me, Nina. Tell me where you hurt."

Some of the pain went back to the genesis of my creation and we sat up and talked about it until Nina-Marie became free. He didn't talk to Nina-Marie the prophetess. He addressed His daughter. Many times you can be so conditioned to being power packed and ready for action that you forget He is concerned about the internal person who you are. He's not interested in the wrapping paper on you but the actual gift that you are. But you have to allow Him to see you as you really are.

That night the Lord used a regular movie to show me what I could not see. In the drama of Miaggi's care for the Kid, I actualized how so much more the Father's care was for me. He reminded me of the passage of Luke 11:13,

If ye then, being evil, know how to give good gifts unto your children: how much more shall your heavenly Father give the Holy Spirit to them that ask Him?

It was one of those hard cries when you don't want anyone else in the room with you. You don't want anyone in your environment because it's personal, intimate, and heart-heavy. Have you ever been in a place in the Spirit when speaking in tongues is not enough? You can name it and claim it and freeze it and frame it but some things in your life and destiny come only in the fullness of time, as all time is appointed by God. When you get through with all of your confessions, God is yet growing you up and developing His character in you.

You are destined for tremendous success. The hand of God is upon your life. The plans of God over you will be fulfilled faster and less painlessly if you go into your secret place and allow Him to "Miaggi" you. I pray that you will.

2

BEFORE THE LAMB WAS SLAIN

There is a time limit for every season in your life. Regardless of how painful, awkward, stressful, or challenging a situation or season might be, it will end! Glory to God the Father! To everything there is a limitation of time. In the beginning, God established provision for you. He anticipated the demise of man's obedience concerning the tree in the Garden, so Christ gave His life for the purposes of redemption.

When the Lamb was slain, provision was permanently established for you. When? In the beginning! God put everything you would ever need in the earth realm. As you get plugged into His divine purposes for your life, the needs surfacing will be met and balanced out by the turning of His hand over your life.

Revelations 13:8 tells us that Christ was the Lamb slain from the foundation of the world. Before God stepped into the nothingness of space and instituted the processes of creation, the Lamb was slain.

Before you could ever need salvation, the Lamb was slain. Before you could ever need healing, the Lamb was slain. Before you could ever need deliverance, the Lamb was slain. He began the process of pulling you into redemption before you could even get here to mess up. That is what I call anticipating provision!

One day in a moment we can't define, there was a conclave in heaven. God the Father, God the Son, and God the Holy Ghost were present. God the Father said, "I'm going to make man and man is going to sin." God the Son said, "I love man so I will die to pay the price for his sin. Then I'll be back." God the Holy Ghost said, "I will teach man and always lead him in the direction that points him back to the Father."

They were all in agreement so the meeting adjourned. If you can, imagine this scene:

A colossal white wall so bright it stuns your senses. A white so white it blinds you and causes you to turn in another direction. A huge beautiful blinding white wall, cut, etched, and carved in purpose. As you approach the white wall, you take a peek behind it.

Far in the distance, you can barely make out some type of high ledge. As you walk closer, it becomes clear that what you see is an altar. Upon this altar you see the soft curly hair of a little white lamb.

You think, "Oh how precious! That little lamb must have gotten lost from the crowd and is taking a nap. Maybe it's waiting to be rescued." Then as you continue going closer, on the pristine white altar, you see another color.

Your curiosity causes you to walk a little bit faster. As you draw closer to the walled stone altar, you see a thick line of vivid color running down the altar. Then for the first time, you notice the lamb is motionless. You're almost running now. You're panting and short of breath, wanting to be closer to see, but not wanting your suspicions confirmed by sight. This can't be what you think it is. As you are now in full view of the altar, you know what has happened, but your mind is in denial.

As you approach the altar standing full faced in front of it, you can now see the full scene. The precious little lamb is dead. His throat is slit left to right, his wool matted and forever stained crimson in color, and you smell the heavy stench of warm just-killed blood as it runs down the altar wall. All life has ebbed from his little body. He is dead. His purpose has been fulfilled.

God made provision for you, even before He made you so that in the fullness of time, when you stood in the moment of the now with Him, everything needed to fulfill your destiny would already have been paid for. Christ in you, the hope of glory, is the ongoing assurance that "it" will be completed. Now you need to define your "it."

For every moment in which you stand, you have what I have termed a "grace gifting coverage." For every assigned space of time in your destined life, you have grace gifting to get through it. This means you have the grace to complete and fulfill that particular assignment. There is divine authorization, divine provision, and divine protection for you when you are in the moment, or the place in time, that God desires you to be in.

You are not suffering certain hardships, experiencing certain challenges, and dealing with certain devils just because. It is a part of the plan of God over your life and it will work out for your good. If you don't believe that, you can put this book down. You can put it in your junk drawer and go watch television. You must understand that God is large and in charge. He knows what He is doing even when it looks like He's fumbling the ball.

Your father and mother had to come together at a specific moment so that you would be this age right now, to be a part of this present moment and not a part of history. The details surrounding your birth may not have been societally perfect, but then again neither were Christ's. Yet He fulfilled His life's assignment and so must you. Jesus came in the form of spermatozoa through the Holy Ghost. Can you imagine that? God the Father placed the Glory of Heaven into the womb of a mortal woman. When Jesus came into the earth as a human, immortality was placed into mortality. He placed boundless into limited. He put life into a container that would die, knowing full well that the temporal death would bring forth eternal life. He did all that for you. So you must go forth and accomplish all that has been assigned to you in the Spirit.

3

PROPHETIC PREMISES

One day, the Lord dropped a little niggling in my spirit concerning Hebrews 13:8.

I kept hearing, "The same yesterday, today, and forever. Yesterday. Today. Forever. The same yesterday. The same today. The same forever. The same, the same. the same." I heard these sayings over and over again.

One of the premise passages for this writing is found in Hebrews 13:8,

Jesus Christ the same yesterday, and today, and forever.

This might sound like a very basic passage but it is a life-changing premise. As a part of the Godhead, Jesus was present in Genesis 1:1 in those first four words, *In the beginning, God.* He was present then, and He is present right now because He is eternal. He has no point of origin, thus He has no point of cessation.

Time is a measure of life. Time is also a gift. Time is a privilege. Time is a discipline. Time is a miracle. Time provides opportunities for miracles and healings. If you are in pain or in a horror season, time can seem cruel and crusty. But the time of suffering will end. All time is born of God. The way you spend it, treat it, and appropriate it is solely dependent on you. It is your responsibility. The decisions you make in this season will affect the next 12-15 years of your life so it is of utmost importance that you make the right decisions.

In order for Jesus to die, He first had to be born. In order for Him to be born, He first had to be planted in Mary's womb on a certain day, so that He could come forth on a certain day. He had to be certain ages physically for certain things to happen spiritually that would affect us dimensionally. And so it goes. As it was with Christ, so it is with you and me.

In the beginning God. In the beginning God. What did God do in the beginning? He supplied everything you would ever need. God made a ransom and then Jesus met it. When? In the beginning. Why? Because in the beginning God was on the scene. He was the scene! The scene was comprised of Who He was and today it is comprised of Who He is. Who is He in your life?

The great poet James Weldon Johnson writes in "The Creation" that God stepped out in space. In all actuality, God defined space by His existence because where He stood, there was. The place where He did not stand became space. Because He stood everywhere, man just named it anyway. Everything is defined by God's very existence. Because He is everywhere all of the time, space and time are locked up in Him.

Yesterday was the time before this present day and tomorrow is the time that will proceed the moment we're in now. Whether you're cognizant and wake, whether you're in travail, whether you're asleep, whether things are working out the way you want them to or not, God wants you to actualize that He is in control.

You are standing in the moment of the now and like happiness, wind, or breath, this moment cannot be captured, only felt and experienced. In the moment, there is no room for failure, mediocrity, or superfluous drama. All energies are spent on the precious commodity of obedience. In this moment there is room for progression, growth, hope, and faith. There is delineation of purpose. But it's only in the moment. The moment is precision. The moment is predicated on decision. The moment must not be lost in derision.

Many Christians struggle on conscious, unconscious, and subconscious levels with the fear of failure but even more with the fear of success. We are reminded in 1 John 4:18 that, *There is no fear in love; but perfect love casteth out fear: because fear hath torment.*

You may easily shrug it off and say, "Yes, I was afraid but I've been delivered. Praise the Lord!" But then you continue to evade the success that Christ died for you to walk in. Sometimes people fear success because it connotates responsibility. It connotates exposure, notoriety, and a public lifestyle. God has made you the head and not the tail, therefore you are legitimately authorized. You have been commanded to walk in success even as you stretch and grow in your spirit man. So walk in that honor.

Where are you standing right now in this moment of your life? Are you standing in a time of refreshing or in a time of consecration? Are you in a place of reconciliation, or in the valley of decision? Maybe God is calling you, beckoning you, and pulling you to Himself for a season, requiring more holiness to be produced in the fruit of your life.

Where are you standing in this moment of time? Maybe He's pulling you slowly but surely in quiet and in confidence (Isaiah 30:15). Is He wooing you into another dimension in Him? Is He pulling you into a new place of fasting, a new place in reading His Word, a new place in studying His Word, and into a new place of separation and pause?

In the moment of the now is reconciliation. In the moment of the now is rejuvenation. In the moment of the now is restoration. In the moment of the now is resurrection. In the moment of the now is redemption.

We now have access to the redemption of time. What are the things of your past that attempt to hold you with the graying, calloused claws of failure or guilt? In the moment of the now, Christ stands to redeem you and everything attached to you but you must allow Him entrance to redeem. He wants to redeem not only your sinful nature, but even the redemption of your past. From antiquity (time ancient) to perpetuity (time immemorial), Christ in you, the Hope of Glory, stands ready to redeem all of the time in your life. All you have to do is allow Him.

It is the desire of darkness that you live in the past. Why? Because it's a place to which you have no legal access or entrance. If you are in the past, you had better run for your life. You have no permission or authorization to be there!

The major premise of this book is the third chapter of the book of Ecclesiastes,

. . .*He hath made every thing beautiful in His time: also He hath set the world in their heart, so that no man can find out the work that God maketh from the beginning to the end.*

. . .*I know that, whatsoever God doeth, it shall be forever: nothing can be put to it, nor anything taken from it: and God doeth it, that men should fear before Him.*

. . .*That which hath been is now; and that which is to be hath already been; and God requireth that which is past.*

. . .*For there is a time for every purpose and every work.*

Whether you're standing in yesterday, last night, this morning, or the tomorrow of your life, Jesus Christ, the same yesterday, today, and forever, desires total accessibility to every reference of time that you can connotate, dredge up, or pull up on the data banks of your mind.

Hebrews 13:8 tells us that Jesus Christ is the same, non-changing, perpetual, consistent, steadfast, unmovable. When? Yesterday. Really? Yes. But wait, He's not finished. He's also the same today and forever. Regardless of what you are going through, He'll be with you forever.

Many times we want Jesus to rescue us. We get Jesus confused with Superman. "Look! Up in the air! It's a bird, it's a plane. No, it's Super Jesus! Bouncing faster than a faith check, flying higher than your dreams, it's Super Jesus!" As Lois Lane was screaming and falling, Superman would be fast on his way to her rescue. He would sweep through the air and catch Lois just before she hit the cement.

You could feel the emotional release and breathe a sigh of relief as he swept her into his arms. Oh, how awesome he was! As a child, I never could figure out why if she really was falling, her hair wasn't blowing straight up? If she was falling down, why didn't her dress didn't fly up. I guess that's why my brother said, "Nina girl, you think too much!"

We have been societally conditioned to supernatural rescue. When crisis strikes and life is awry, we expect the same from Jesus. However, there have been times in my life when not only did Jesus not catch me, He let me splatter all over the place.

Anyone could have caught Humpty Dumpty but only the King could put him back together again. The Lord allowed me to splatter but it was only so He could raise me and get all of the glory from my crash. Only He could repair me so seamlessly. When we "fix" ourselves, people can always tell it was a "self-job." We know you did it yourself because we see your ear on your knee and your hand coming out of your shoulder and your eye in your mouth. When you allow the Holy Spirit to repair you, the crash becomes a stepping stone to greatness in the fullness of time.

In the fullness of His divine time, He has used my personal crisis to show Himself strong to people in my life and people on the planet. The Lord gave me the title of my next work, "Company in the Fire." I kept praying for a miracle, but He gave me a message. Do you not know that in the hardest moment of their personal fire, Jesus came and stood with Shadrach, Meshach, and Abednego? Notice that He never put the fire out. He came and stood in it with them.

Do you want the fire put out or do you want His company in the flames? I know I would rather Him just put the fire out, but that has never happened in my life. I would be so angry that at times I did not want His company. I felt like, "Jesus, if you really want to do something for me, put this fire out! I don't want to be spiritual and mature and learn deep lessons of faith. I want out!" So in times past, He'd sigh and put the fire out.

Somewhere down the road of my life, there would be moments of spontaneous combustion. Then I would bind the devil, loose angels, stand on the Word, name it and claim it, freeze it and frame it, plead the Blood, pull out the oil, and do everything else that we are taught to do.

The fact was that until I dealt with that issue or passed that specific test, I would forever have to face it. Perhaps it would happen at different points, different times, and with different people in different places, but it was the same test or issue.

Many people think Isaiah 43:2b says we will walk through the fire but when we come out, we won't smell like smoke. The scripture actually states,

When thou walkest through the fire, thou shalt not be burned; neither shall the flame kindle upon thee.

That is a promise that you can stand on. My life is a living, breathing, walking witness of this passage. I have walked through some fire. I felt I would be destroyed but I was not because Jesus was with me.

Jesus is with you forever. His presence does not negate the work you have to fulfill for your destiny. As a matter of fact, it enforces and supports it tremendously. You still have an appointment with destiny. Perhaps you couldn't fulfill a particular assignment in the past. Maybe it was for this particular season.

You certainly can't do it tomorrow because you're not there yet. The acceptable time is now! If God is motioning you in the direction of His perfect will, you can run, but you can't hide! The prophet, priest and King of Israel, David, knew this. Psalms 139:7-10 makes that perfectly clear:

Whither shall I go from thy spirit? Or whither shall I flee from thy presence?

If I ascend up into heaven, thou art there: if I make my bed in hell, behold, thou art there.

If I take the wings of the morning, and dwell in the uttermost parts of the sea;

Even there shall thy hand lead me, and thy right hand shall hold me.

You are not alone. You will never be alone. The presence of the Lord is with you always. You have ministering angels assigned to you who are probably begging for work. You have the promise of the Holy Spirit and the presence of the King. You are royalty destined for greatness and this is the timing of the Lord over your life. Destiny is waiting on you. What are you waiting for?

4

MAKING TIME TO DIE

You are standing in a divine moment with God. The moment of the now is a time slot in which the person in relationship with Christ Jesus recognizes that he or she is standing in a sovereign moment of divinity. That is you and you are standing in a divine moment with God. You and you alone stand in this moment. There's no room for husband, wife, child, parent, friend, pastor, or prayer partner. The attention of heaven is focused upon you for specific purposes and assignments that only you can fulfill.

In the Body of Christ, we are experiencing processes of metamorphosis and ongoing change. God is altering the form of His creation. Just as a master seamstress or tailor takes a garment and begins perfecting the existing creation, so is the move of God in our lives. Sometimes there is an adding to and opening of for the purposes of addition. At other times, there is a taking away and a trimming thereof for the purposes of perimeter and delineation. If you will allow Father God to custom design His call upon your life, you will be the best dressed and stand in a designer original! There is a price to pay for this garment, but rest assured there won't be a knock-off copy to be found.

You are wonderful. You really are. You may not believe it, but you are gifted. You are anointed and you are also capable of more. Not only does heaven believe this concerning you, but provision has been made through the act of love we call Calvary. So you have no excuse or reason to remain the same. You must change.

When Jesus was hanging on the cross, He couldn't wipe His eyes. When the blood was running down His face, and the sweat and other stuff was oozing from the exposure of damaged, exposed layers of tissue, He couldn't even wipe His eyes because His hands were nailed to the cross. But I believe He saw you and He saw me and He nodded in understanding the fullness of His purpose in death.

Because of our humanity, we have a natural and humanistic tendency to think death is the absolute end. In physical aspects, it is. Death is final. Yet our divinity reminds us that physical death is the beginning of a whole new realm of living. We build our faith on the death of Christ, but we don't want to die.

I am reminded of my husband when he began the actual process of dying. In the daytime on that Friday, we were going upstairs to our bedroom. As my foot mounted the first step, I felt something in the spirit shift and move. I really can't tell you what it was because I honestly don't know. All I know is that I felt "us" shift to "me." I cry now just from remembering.

When we walked into our bedroom, he sat on his side of the bed. It took us about 20- 25 minutes to make him comfortable. He was in exquisite agony and discomfort. AIDS will do that to you. I laid in bed next to him and he propped himself on my thigh and went to sleep. I watched the television with a massive lump in my throat.

My heart hurt so badly, my breathing was forced and shallow. Everything in me wanted to grab God's arm and say, "Please don't do this to me. I look a lot stronger than I really am. C'mon now, you know my frame and you know I've just been "faithing" it. Please don't do this to me. Please don't take my husband." But you know what? In all of my poignant, silent dialogue, heaven didn't say crap. Not a doggone thing.

Donn laid on me with his eyes closed. I remember looking into his face and thinking, "Lord this man has brought me so much joy. If I never get loved again, I've been loved right. I was invited to a party and the party was me." He exhaled and I could feel him beginning to let go. Five days later, I was a widow.

Just because five is the number of grace doesn't mean I felt I had the grace to sustain this loss. He had recently told me, "Sweetheart, I'm not really going to die. I'm just going to live on." Looking back, I can see that his focus was the actual going to, as in going from one place to another. It was not the process but the destination.

In the midst of his dying, my husband had an understanding of life on another strata. We only know of life on this terra firma. I believe in that moment, my husband was trying to share with me an understanding that I wasn't ready to process. All I knew was that in order for him to "go to," he first had to leave me. That was the part I could not process. My spirit was telling me what was going on, but my flesh wasn't having it. My triune self still could not process this dichotomy.

Only now am I somewhat comforted and even that is by force. My mom, my sisters, my church, and closest friends have made me know that they hurt with me and for me. Initially I refused heaven's comfort. I was so wounded when I walked in a room, you could literally smell fresh blood in the Spirit. Initially my understanding was vague but my wounds are healing because I am allowing Jesus to complete the work of healing in me. I see through this glass darkly and I'm not even wearing shades.

Jesus is not asking you to die some horrid, violent death.

What He is asking you is to make the decision to die daily to your will, your way, your agenda, your little blueprints, and your itineraries. He only asks that we allow Him to be Lord of our total lives, not just when we mess things up.

I believe in the Garden of Gethsemane, Jesus was saying "Father, I'm tired and I've only been here 33 years. All I've known is miracles and wonders and rejection and betrayal. Surely there has to be a balance. I'm tired of working miracles and then being cast away. I'm tired of being thronged and then left alone."

Are you sure you want to walk in supernatural miracles? There are some realms of anointing that will cost you everything in your life. You'll walk out on stage and thousands will swoon under the anointing of God but when the curtain drops, you must pay the price.

The Apostle Paul speaks frequently and candidly of dying to self. If you are going to do anything in God, if you are going to flow in the Holy Spirit and not some strange spirit, if you are going to risk everything to fulfill the call of God on your life, you will have to die to yourself.

Your worst critic, the person who reminds you of your every failure, the person who flashes fleeting images of you in the throes of sin, is in your mirror. Look at the mirror and command that flesh to die! Christ died once so that we would live forever so why would you be tormented with what you've done, where you did it, and who you did it with or to?

You know that the wages of sin is death and the gift of God is eternal life through Jesus (Romans 6:23). You know the weapons of our warfare are not carnal but mighty through God to the pulling down of strongholds (2 Corinthians 10:4).

You can know all the Word in the world, but if you never forgive yourself, you're still hanging on the cross. Please allow me to inform you that you do not have the grace to sustain

Calvary. If it killed Christ, it would laugh at your mere mortality.

Everything lives and then it dies. Jesus could not even die *forever*. At some point He had to exhale and enter in. As He did, so must you. You cannot wrestle with your issues forever. If you feel too weak, get a covenant friend or kingdom secret keeper who will pray with you and minister to that area of your life. Then be still and know that He is God (Psalm 46:10). You must die to your flesh daily. It's a day-to-day decision.

The anointing of God on your life will cost you relation-ships, friendships, loss of substance, and anything else you care for or about. God is a jealous God and He will not share you, His chosen. You who are His chosen have certain mandates on your life. My father in the Gospel, Dr. Richard Henton says, "Others can but you cannot."

If you are chosen of God, I highly recommend that you call Monument of Faith Church in Chicago and order "God's Chosen Children of Destiny." This is the word that Dr. Henton preached the night the Lord confirmed His selection of my life, as one chosen by God and sent of God. The message launched me out into the deep, sent me forth into ministry, and yet blesses my life today.

5

CONCEPTS OF TIME

We have a tendency in our pluralistic environment to think of time as seconds, minutes, hours, days, weeks, months, years, eons, ad infinitum. But when you study concepts of time, the word means consistent, perpetual, and ongoing.

When you interview for a new position and you return for the third interview and all of your references check out, what does the interviewer say? When they offer you the position, the person is really asking if you will be on time. When he or she asks if will you be on time, they are asking if you are going to be consistent. "Will you be steadfast and unmovable, or will you call in sick when I call in sick?" The questions of time refer to integrity and consistency in your character.

The word "time" is mentioned in the Bible in approximately 599 occurrences. Time is eternal and time is locked up in God. I love to hear Lashun Pace Rhodes sing "My Times Are In His Hands." If you ever want to get free, that'll help do it for you!

Galatians 4:4-5 tells of the fullness of time,

But when the fullness of the time was come, God sent forth His Son made of a woman, made under the law,

To redeem them that were under the law, that we might receive the adoption of sons.

Ecclesiastes 3:1 tells us,

To every thing there is a season, a time to every purpose under the heaven.

To reference the concept of time, we begin by defining it. To walk in the knowledge or awareness of anything, you must first grasp the understanding of what it is, and it's application in your life to appropriately fulfill it's purpose in your life.

Two references for time are the words *Chronos* and *Kairos*.

Chronos is the measurement of time. It's the succession of moments as time continues on or continues passing. *Chronos* is time as we know it, the measurement of seconds, minutes, hours, days, months, years, decades, etc. It is the logistical concept of time or the recording of minutes multiplied and added to.

Kairos is the divine opportunity of time. It is that which time affords or allows you to do. What *Kairos* are you doing with your *Chronos?* What opportunities are you taking advantage of with the time allotted unto you? God is not requiring you to be the next Katherine Kuhlman or A.A. Allen. He wants you to be you. He is requiring you to be the fullness of you in this hour.

As *Kairos* references the most opportune time, it becomes the moment of opportunity. It refers to seasons at which preordained events *need* to take place, not *take* place. There is a tremendous difference in what needs to be done versus what will be done. Pray today that the Lord's will be done.

Sometimes it is needful that the heavens become as brass in your life. It causes you to search and cry out to God. Sometimes humanity gets a little too familiar with divinity and temporary silence is the result. When you call and He doesn't come running, you pause and double check. Then if you still do not receive a response, you begin to seek Him with purpose and on purpose.

As a child playing in the house, you knew Mom was in the kitchen because you could hear the pots and pans and cooking action. So you stayed in the room playing or watching the cowboy movies. After a bit you noticed a little silence. If it continued, everything you were doing lessened in importance. You went to see where Mom was. Maybe you would find her at the back of the pantry where she couldn't hear you. Or perhaps she had gone to put a load of clothes in the dryer. When she turned around almost bumping into you, she would ask what you wanted and the world famous reply was, "Uh, nothing."

What you actually meant was, "Where were you? What were you doing? Why did you get quiet? Did you leave me? Was I alone for a minute? Are you really watching me? Aren't I the center of your attention? You're not leaving me, are you?" Fear of abandonment quietly slipped back down and you resumed your game or movie. All was well because Mom was around. It is the same way with God. He will never leave you nor forsake you. But in the times you begin to take His presence for granted, do not be surprised by sudden silence. He is a jealous God and He wants your attention.

When you become convinced that God knew what He was doing when He made you, you're going to be straight. You must realize that God was not on a break or drinking coffee when your dust came up. Heaven is convinced that you are ready to step into the fullness of God's plans for your life and destiny. Your greatest struggle is with yourself!

I believe the sages and prophets of old are what Joyce Landorf called "balcony people." I believe Nahum, Obadiah, Daniel and David lean over the balconies of glory and urge us on. I believe when every devil in hell is lying on you and plotting your demise, Elisha and Elijah are saying, "Look at Debra struggle. Look at Irene holding on! Remember when we went through that? Remember when we felt like we were the only ones trying to do the right thing?" I believe the apostles and prophets of old are prototypes for us today. If they made it, you can and will make it! To arrive at the pinpoint of destiny, you must stay out of yesterday. You have no legal access into your yesterday because you are born of God and you do not have to walk in illegal or illegitimate places. Let God handle your yesterdays.

The Word of God tell us in Isaiah 43:18-19,

Remember ye not the former things, neither consider the things of old.

Behold, I will do a new thing; now it shall spring forth; shall ye not know it? I will even make a way in the wilderness, and rivers in the desert.

2 Thessalonians 1:6-7a tells us the time of toil ends in rest,

Seeing it is a righteous thing with God to recompense tribulation to them that trouble you;

And to you who are troubled . . . rest with us.

Romans 8: 17-18 tells us that the time of suffering ends in glory,

And if children, then heirs; heirs of God, and joint heirs with Christ; if so be that we suffer with him, that we may also be glorified together.

For I reckon that the sufferings of this present time are not worthy to be compared with the glory which shall be revealed in us.

Habakkuk 2:2 tells us the vision is for an appointed time, which means the vision is not for what? The moment. It is for an appointed time. I think it's very interesting that God creates things in terms of spheres. Many things that God creates are cyclitic or move in cycles of time. Look at your watch. The design or face might be square but the movement is erpetual, circular. When a man and woman come together in covenant union, the token or symbol is the wedding ring. Why? Because it has no beginning and it has no end. It has no point of entrance and no point of exit. That is the concept of time in God.

When was the world formulated? We can look at geographical charts and search different studies or look at the rings in a redwood tree. But time was created when God made the decision to create it. When did God make the decision to create time? When God decided to create time. When was the beginning of time? When God decided to create time. It still goes in that circle.

Out of the time in circles, we come to experience the denotation of the seasons — winter, spring, summer, and fall. Even within each of those seasons, there are still other seasons. In summer, you have what we loosely term "Indian summer."

Where are you standing in your moment of the now? Jesus Christ is the same, continual, perpetual, permanent, Ancient of Days, today, in your moment, forever, everlasting, and ongoing. Where are you and what are you doing? What season are you standing in? Are you in winter, a time of incubation and isolation? Do you find yourself on the inside looking out at the others having fun and frolicking? Are you yearning and desiring to get out "there" but it's not been your season? There are seasons in your life. You can control them or you can let God. He can determine the barometric pressure and set the climate control, too.

You might find yourself with a new hunger. What do you really want? I don't know but I've got to have it now! What are you craving? Maybe it's time for some prostration with some fasting on the side. Maybe it's time for some separation so that carnality can't abide. Maybe you just want to slip away and lay on the floor and worship. What are you hungering for in your spirit?

You know what time it is in your life? It's time for an appetite change. The Father has created a menu for you and you alone. The portions are exactly what you need and you will leave satisfied. There is a predetermination already made that when you keep saying yes to God, you get to another point and place in Him. In that place, there is a set time for you to get hungry for more of Him.

There will be moments when other cravings and desires manifest and announce themselves. Because of the laws of God and the Kingdom, some must go unmet until all things are prepared for you. Until that time, feed those needs from the Word of God.

To experience ongoing life is to experience change.

1 Corinthians 1:51-52 says,

Behold, I show you a mystery;

We shall not all sleep, but we shall all be changed in a moment, in the twinkling of an eye, at the last trump: for the trumpet shall sound, and the dead shall be raised incorruptible, but we shall be changed.

When will we be changed? In a moment.

Look at the seasons of your life. Which season do you believe you are standing in today? You might be standing in the hot August heat of change. Even though the water is pleasant, it's dry and the light bearing down on you might be more than you would choose to take at any given moment. Maybe you look or seek the shelter of a shade covering because the light is so bright. Maybe the searchlight of the Holy Ghost is shining so on you, revealing to you those areas He desires to strengthen and corrupt, and you feel like saying, "Give me some sunglasses. Give me a break!"

Do you remember what I call "hot alter prayers?" You stand at the alter and say, "Oh, have your way, God. Move by Your Spirit. Shake me up and clean me out." He says, "Okay. Sure" and He begins the process. Then you say, "God, the light is too bright" but you are the one who said, "Let Your glory be revealed in me." As He begins the process of creation in us, we have the tendency as mortals to change our minds.

Maybe you are in the Autumn of your life. The kids are going back to school, the activity in the neighborhood has quieted down, and the college kids have gone away. Things are kind of peaceful and this peace causes you to feel restless. You see everyone going off in pivotal directions and moving to different purposes. You might be a housewife at home, watching all the change and feeling a bit left out or isolated. You might think, "Even the kids are moving in purpose. He's in Head Start and she's in school. My husband has gone to work and, Lord, I'm just sitting here. How long do I have to sit here? I'm bored. I should be doing something."

Are you in the Autumn season today? This is a beautiful, colorful season as the leaves begin the process of dying. When they are full of life, they are green, full of chlorophyll. As they begin to lose the essence, the process of discoloration begins. There is beauty in death. There is beauty in dying.

I had in 1980 a little blueprint for my life. I wanted my bachelor degree finished that year, my masters in two years, and wedged in at some point between the two, I wanted God to provide a husband. Two and a half years after getting married, we'd have a child. Then I would enter a doctoral program and maybe in a year have a second child. By the time the first child was through, we'd begin putting money on a home. I had a ridiculous blueprint. I thought it was perfect but my ways did not line up with His because Isaiah 55 tell us, *My ways are not your ways, and my thoughts are higher than your thoughts.* When you submit yourself to God, the way up is down. When you submit yourself to Him, you begin to take on His mind.

When people ask, "What are you going to do?" and you answer, "I don't know, let me pray about it," you are actually saying, "Let me go before God and get the mind of God over this situation." There is nothing in your life so minute that the Father does not direct impartation. There is no situation in your life so small that He does not desire to speak into it. We have a tendency to make things critical or insurmountable insignificancies. Yet, from the least to the greatest, He wants influence in your moment.

You might be standing in Lo-debar, the valley of decision. You might be standing in a place of weeping. You might be standing today making determinations that will affect the balance of who you are. Where are you in the moment of the now?

There are those who would say, "I understand the will of God for my life, I think I understand His purpose, and I'm beginning to tap into it, but. . . ." There is always a "but." I used to tell the Lord, "I'll be Your prophet, *but* I'm young. I'll be Your speaker, *but* I'm single, I don't have a covering. I'll be Your messenger all over the world *but. . . .*" You can use your ethnocentrism, your marital status, your childlessness, or the fact that you have many children. You can use geographical excuses or educational excuses such as, "Well, I'm not as smart as he is. I'm not as well read." Get that but out of the way and allow God to rule and reign in your moment.

The Word says we shall be changed in a moment. We who are engraved or engrafted into the body of Jesus Christ, adopted by royal lineage, no longer servants but family now, can allow Jesus to live in us. The mind of Christ is activated in you because you've transformed your mind by taking on His mind. Your mind is transformed by the dunamus of the Word of God and because He is in you, you alone are enough to detonate in any environment. Because His power is released in you, your being in the situation changes.

There is a time limit to every season of your life. Regardless of how painful, awkward, stressful, or challenging a situation might be, it will end! To every thing there is a limitation of time. In the beginning, God made provision for you. He anticipated the demise of man's obedience concerning the tree, so Christ gave His life for the purposes of redemption.

Remember this from Chapter Two: when the Lamb was slain, provision was permanently established for you. When? In the beginning! God put everything you would ever need in the earth realm. As you get plugged into His purposes for your life, the needs surfacing will be met and balanced out by His provision. One of the provision benefits you received was for covering.

When you shop for clothing there is a room provided to cover you as you change from one outfit of clothing to another. When you step out of the little booth, you have transformed your attire. Much like this, the Holy Spirit "covers" us or provides divine coverage as we experience the process of dimensional transformation.

If you have the anointing to do a certain thing or accomplish a specific task, no matter how fast your heart beats, your knees knock, or your palms sweat, you must stay in your moment. You have coverage because Christ was made naked. On the tree of Calvary, they stripped Him and embarrassed Him in order that you would receive the benefits.

God is looking for a people who will be made naked for Him. He is looking for people who will allow Him and others to see their scars and afford Him entrance into their secret chambers at His personal convenience. God is looking for a naked man and a naked woman who He can show Himself strong through. God is looking for a people who will wear gossamer garments through which their vulnerabilities will be shown.

You are now naked and disrobed of every opportunity to lie down and be nothing, You are stripped of the things that would hold you back from the fulfillment of who you are.

You are going places in the Holy Ghost. You are going places in the Spirit. You are going to change. You are going to prosper. You are going to grow.

There's nothing the devil or anyone else can do about it because God has made a choice of you and you are special. You haven't even believed it and you haven't always understood why your life was so hard and things were always so heavy but other people and other things knew who you were. That's why they could not and would not celebrate you. Destiny is a party where you are the guest of honor.

Who wants to be naked? No one! Why not? Because when we are naked, you can see our bruises and places of shame. No one wants to be naked. To be disrobed is to be disgraced. Many times we associate nakedness with shame and embarrassment.

Shame's place of origin is found in Genesis 1:7-8,

And the eyes of them both were opened, and they knew that they were naked; and they sewed fig leaves together, and made themselves aprons.

And they heard the voice of the Lord God walking in the garden in the cool of the day: and Adam and his wife hid themselves from the presence of the Lord God amongst the trees of the garden.

Since Christ accomplished Calvary, we can lose our shame based nature and command lying spirits of degradation to be silenced in the Name of Jesus. It is now time for you to lose the haunting spirits of shame that have followed you until now. Expose them! Shine the light of God on them! Command them to go in the Name of Jesus. Resist satan and he will flee.

Many things that I have dealt with in life were a direct result of me not wanting to be uncovered. All of my natural life, I had hated confrontation. I absolutely ran from it, hid from it, and did whatever was necessary to get away from it. I liked being easy going, sweet, and approachable. I portrayed my strengths and hid my weaknesses out of shame.

I clearly remember a season about 15 years ago in my itinerant ministry when I had to deal with strong spirits of disrespect. Of course it was easier to just say, "It's the devil" and I'm sure it was. But that wasn't the point the Spirit of the Lord kept showing me. I believe I exacerbated that particular grace. I remember the Holy Spirit dealing firmly with me about this.

I was whining (some of you call it prayer) and I told the Lord I was tired of being disrespected and discounted. If you have ever fulfilled any destiny time in ministry, you have scars to prove it. The Lord really hurt my feelings. He told me, "I have given you an ear to hear me and a mind to make right decisions. I have given you a mouth to voice yourself on this earth and your tongue is the pen of a ready writer. I have given you everything you need to combat this spirit. You are being disrespected because you let people disrespect you." Then He became silent and that is all He has said about that matter to this day.

When the situation came before me again, it was in the Spirit. I had an open eye vision of a meeting that was called. It was a diabolical set up to destroy a person. In the vision, I was standing in a corner of the room watching people and listening to the discussion. Then I heard a knock on the door. A brother in Christ who once was my brother in relationship, answered that knock. Then I saw myself walking into this room. I almost passed out in the vision, watching it happen.

Then, like a movie, there was a freeze frame. The Holy Spirit gave me an inner something that I had never had before.

I knew whatever it was, it was from God. I came into the room, stood behind one of the executive chairs, and put my hands on the shoulders of the chair. In the Word of God, the shoulders often represent the place of strength.

As I stood, I looked into the eyes of each person in the room. Heads began to drop and people began to flip through notes. They could not maintain eye contact. It was like when Jesus wrote in the dirt and people began to drift away (John 8:1-11).

I stood up straight, posture erect, and said to no one in particular and everyone in general, "Never again will I be disrespected, or played a nickel for a dime. If you approach me, it must be in respect or you will not stand before me. If you confront me, you must be prepared to be confronted and put on the stand. If you come to take me down, you should come wearing sweats. You may not like me or care for my personality but you will respect me or not abide in my space."

As I spoke, I began to cry. As I cried, I could feel strength and understanding coursing through my blood. I felt healing and anger and sorrow and joy. When it was finished, I laid before the Lord. He spoke softly to me. He told me healing came because I had finally takin a stand that was long overdue.

The anger was the betrayal of people I love, the sorrow was having found myself manipulated by others, and the joy was that it had finally been dealt with in the Spirit and not just in the strength of my flesh.

I would love to say it has not happened since, but that would be a lie. But it is peaceful to say the few times that it has happened, I clearly and firmly let people know that I am available and personally able to introduce them to the Creator of the Universe!

Some other references for time include these words:

Ad is a masculine noun that means duration, perpetuity, and eternity. It denotes the unforeseeable future. It appears 19 times in the Bible. *Ad* is time denoting the unforeseeable future.

Owlam is a Hebrew noun that means time passed. It references time or duration which is hidden to the vanishing point! This appears 440 times in the Bible.

Owlam makes me think of the arrival of God in Genesis One. I should say the announcement of God. When God stepped out in creation, He just began to be there, because He already was and is and will be. He had not just arrived there. He was there already because He is the I Am. He didn't come on the scene, He was the scene, and still is.

Alam is the Aramaic noun equivalent of *owlam*. It means the remote time from antiquity (time past) to perpetuity (time future or time to come). This usually refers to either your yesterday or your tomorrow.

If you failed yesterday or 20 years ago, you are yet liable to fulfill the purposes of God over your life. You might say, "Well, you don't understand." Perhaps not, but you still must fulfill destiny. I don't care if you killed a killer, caught a crook, or fell like Humpty Dumpty.

I don't care if your father was a bum and his father was a bum and his father was a bum. It does not automatically mean that you have to be a bum. If you are a bum, it's because that's what you want to be. The Word of God, the Name of Jesus, and the Blood of Jesus is stronger than any generational curse!

You are mandated to walk in greatness and you must. We acknowledge a fall. All have sinned and come short, some shorter than others, but we allow Jesus to go into that moment and redeem it. We call this prophetic disclosure. Prophetic disclosure is not psychic, eerie, or spooky. It's the simple fact that the Godhead transcends everything we know. God can redeem absolutely anything. A fall is not the end. It's the end of a flesh-governed moment and the beginning of a new chapter in Jesus. We serve the chance-again God.

Another concept of time is *eth*. It is the right time, the proper time, a short-lived season. The vicissitudes of events in your life.

There are three general concepts of *eth* in your life:

1. The regular time
2. The appropriate time
3. A set time

Circumstances in your life can happen in any of these frame references, but your decisions to hear and obey God can only happen in the frame references that you select. What realm of *eth* are you living in? Is it determined by you or the Holy Ghost?

There are events in your life that can happen at any given moment, and that moment can be the right time. Have you ever been in the right place, but at the wrong time? Have you ever been in the right place and you were too early or you were too late? At any rate, you missed your connection.

There was a time in Christendom when we would miss God. Because of the affordability of time, maybe in two or five or even 10 years, that same thing would come around again. In 1973, I missed God. I made a decision that caused me to miss God in a major way. It took nine years for that thing to come around again. I almost aborted my destiny by taking too long to make a certain decision.

When you miss God, you alter the creation. Do you not realize that it is already perfect if He made it? That's why the Word of God tells us that we are complete in Him. It's not of us, or we could glory in the knowledge. We must choose to mature and endure the processes of maturation. Will you allow God to finish what He has started in you? He has begun the good work in you, now just be still!

You can miss everything available to you in the earth and in the Spirit to be in the moment of the now. You cannot afford to miss God. That is a luxury not found in the budget of the chosen. You can't get that on a layaway plan!

We all know people who started out in God and were spiritually awesome. That person's ministry blew your mind and brought healing to your life. Then maybe you heard that person again in a couple of years and you thought, "Well, maybe tonight was just an off night." Then when you hear them again, it's the same thing. You are witnessing a lawful thing in an illegitimate moment.

You must be careful to enjoy a relationship with Jesus but never allow yourself to become familiar with Him. Because that anointed person was flowing in a particular vein and riding a specific wave, they exchanged tomorrow for today. You cannot stay in today forever!

It's like going to the museum and seeing the glass encasement around the monolithic dinosaurs. They were once the epitome of vicious fierceness. As the earth began to change, other creatures began to adapt but the dinosaur was big, bad, and tough. He didn't change. So when the Ice Age rolled in, he was frozen and fossilized in fierceness. Impotent strength and paralyzed muscles cannot be used to destroy yokes of bondage.

You must continually seek the Lord. Deuteronomy 4:29 tells us, *When you seek me with your whole heart, then I will be found of you.* Greatness is in you. The Word of the Lord comes to your potential.

Like a baby, your destiny is sustained by the umbilical cord of your covenant relationship with Jesus. If you sustain injury, a team of specialists must come and repair the damage to the connection. The Godhead represents the specialists who are there to redeem and repair. If there is damage to the connection, the specialist must come in or the baby (or the vision) will die. At all costs, the baby must live!

Greatness is in you. You need to announce it when you awaken in the morning. When your feet hit the floor, the devil should know he's got trouble on his hands. When your eyes open, hell should become depressed. When you throw that first leg over the bed and your foot hits the floor, the devil should know it's over, even before it's began.

Instead of running from the enemy, the Word of God tells us in James 4:7 to resist him and he will flee. It doesn't say he might flee. It says he will flee. When adversity comes running your way, you should walk towards it knowing that your God is greater.

It matters not if the challenge has on gym shoes or combat boots. Christ in you, the hope of glory is greater. You have the power of the Greater One activated on the inside of you. You should walk up on the challenge, thump your chest, and say as they say in the "hood," "You want some of this!"

He then limps to go tell his imps, "Now you can't get him so go mess with his car." The D.I.T.'s (demons in training) say, "No, let's get him." Then satan has to tell them, "You cannot defeat Dwight or David. You can't make Terry trip. You can't make Frank fall. You cannot master Michael or Marvin. But you can grate their nerves real good. You can try to annoy the fruit of the Spirit out of them but they won't fall."

While you're sipping your morning decaf, darkness is planning an attack on your day.

Let's talk about *Kairos*. *Kairos* is that which time gives opportunity to do, thus an opportune time. *Kairos* is the necessity of the task at hand.

There are certain foreordained events in your life that need to take place and they need to occur at specific, designated times, for the purposes of God to be fulfilled in your life.

6

YOUR YESTERDAY —
GET OUT AND STAY OUT!

The three major Western religions are Christianity, Judaism, and Islam. Their different theologies and belief systems all structurally negate one another. They only agree on one thing — that God created time. Out of all the varied opinions, scriptural tenets, personal premises, and diversified denominations comes this agreement of truth: all time is born of God.

Hebrews 13:8 says, *Jesus Christ the same yesterday, and today, and forever.* This is a basic passage but if you get it in your spirit, it can change your life. As a part of the Godhead, Jesus was present in Genesis 1:1 in those first four words, *In the beginning, God.* He was present then, and He's present right now because He is eternal. He has no point of origin, thus no point of cessation.

Yesterday was the time before this present day and tomorrow is the time that will proceed the moment we're in now. Whether you're cognizant and wake, whether you're in travail, whether you're asleep, whether things are working out the way you want them to or not, God wants you to actualize that He is in control.

We are standing in the moment of the now. Like happiness,

wind, or breath it cannot be captured, only felt and experienced. In the moment, there is no room for failure, mediocrity, or drama. All energies are spent on the precious commodity of obedience. In this moment there is room for progression, growth, hope, and faith. There is delineation of purpose only in the moment.

You cannot help but embrace the moment of the now because it is the place where your provision exists. In the beginning, Father God made provision for any and every thing you will ever need. He doesn't wait until you need bread to grow wheat. He doesn't wait until you're completely parched to give you an old fashioned gully-washing. He anticipates your needs and meets them before you notice their absence.

You may be a person who believes, "Well yes, I do know that greatness is in me and destiny has been released in me. But I can't embrace and fulfill destiny because in one of my yesterdays, I made a mistake. I would step out and take the risk but in 1969 I missed God. In 1973 I messed up. I once thought I heard God and I acted on it and things fell through. I can't take another risk like that."

At some point in time we have all missed God. If you say you haven't, then you just did. We have tried to follow God and at times we have missed it. Perhaps you were afraid and lagged too far behind. Maybe you were excited and got ahead. Maybe you overslept and missed it altogether. You can still fulfill the call of God upon your life.

The enemy will lie and tell you it's too late. He is a liar and the father of lies. One of his most noted achievements is his prowess as a liar. So you cannot believe a liar or his lie. Many Christians struggle on conscious and unconscious levels not only with the fear of failure but also with the fear of success. God's Word reminds us in 1 John 4:18, . . . *There is no fear in love; but perfect love casteth out fear: because fear hath torment.*

You may easily shrug it off and say, "Yes, I was afraid but I've been delivered. Praise the Lord!" But then you continue to evade the success that Christ died for you to walk in. Sometimes people fear success because it connotates responsibility. It connotates exposure, notoriety, and an incredibly public lifestyle.

God has made you the head and not the tail. Therefore, you are legitimate and authorized to succeed. In the words of Dr. Henton, "You've been deputized!" If you have any type of calling on your life, you need to contact Higher Dimensions Ministries and order the 1994 Azusa video series.

Someone once asked me why I am always promoting other people instead of my own product. I really do believe the Word of God. The Word of God tells us that, *A man's gift maketh room for him and brings him before great men.* It does not say a man's publicist or marketing analyst ensures his anointing, notoriety, or name on the earth. I have always been nudged by God to introduce people to other people. Some call it networking. I call it an act of obedience.

In each instance, a portion of their destiny was in their connection. If I know something is excellent and will aid my spiritual development, give me two; one to have and one to share. The things that I suggest to you have blessed my life in ways too deep to comprehend. I believe these suggested materials will seriously bless you.

Where are you standing right now in this moment of your life? Are you standing in a time of refreshing or maybe in a time of consecration? Are you in a place of reconciliation, or in a valley of decision? Maybe God is calling you, beckoning you, and pulling you to Himself for a season. He might be requiring more holiness to be produced in the fruit of your life.

Where are you standing in this moment of time? Maybe

He's pulling you slowly but surely in quiet and in confidence (Isaiah 30:15). Is He wooing you into another dimension in Him? Is He pulling you into a new place of fasting, a place in reading and studying His Word, a place of separation and pause?

In the moment of the now is the redemption of time. What are the things of your past that attempt to hold you with failure or guilt. In the moment of the now, Christ stands to redeem you. Not only the redemption of your sinful nature, but even the redemption of your past. From antiquity (time ancient) to perpetuity (time immemorial), Christ in you, the Hope of Glory, stands ready to redeem time in your life.

It is the desire of darkness that you live in the past. Why? Because it's a place to which you have no legal access or entrance. If you are in the past, you had better run for your life. You have no permission or authorization to be there!

Ecclesiastes 3:11, 14-15, 17b tells us,

. . .*He hath made every thing beautiful in His time: also He hath set the world in their heart, so that no man can find out the work that God maketh from the beginning to the end.*

. . .*I know that, whatsoever God doeth, it shall be forever: nothing can be put to it, nor anything taken from it: and God doeth it, that men should fear before Him.*

. . .*That which hath been is now; and that which is to be hath already been; and God requireth that which is past.*

. . .*For there is a time for every purpose and every work.*

Whether you're standing in yesterday, last night, this morning or the tomorrow of your life, Jesus Christ Who is the same yesterday, today, and forever desires total accessibility to every reference of time that you can connotate, dredge up, or pull up on the data banks of your mind.

You have an appointment with destiny. You couldn't fulfill

your assignment in the past because it's for this particular season. You certainly can't do it tomorrow. The time is now. If God is motioning you in the direction of His perfect will, you can run, but you can't hide! Read Psalms 139:7-10. You cannot hide from God, even cloaked in your past. Yesterday is an address which you have moved from. Your negative yesterdays are a building that has been condemned. It is dangerous and unsafe so get out and stay out!

7

OBEDIENCE IN THE MOMENT

In standing in the eternal now, there is no excuse for failure. There is only room for progression. In the eternal now is delineation of purpose. As a new believer, it was a struggle to determine which voice was God versus your conscious or your own intellect. As you grew and matured and formed a relationship with Him, you began to know His voice from anyone else's. Now you hear God. You hear Him clearly. Now you must begin to obey what He speaks to you. Obedience is of utmost importance.

When I was seven years old, the Spirit of the Lord spoke to me while I was sitting in class. When He called my name, I knew it was His voice. I was familiar with His voice versus my head voice because He had been speaking to me from a very young age. My most vivid memory of the Father talking to me was at about the age of two so when He spoke to me that day in class, it was not unusual.

This time He said, "Nina, I want you to be my prophet." I said, "Okay. Now what's a prophet?" He said, "Sometimes I'm going to tell you things and I want you to say what I say. I'll tell you things for people and you'll say them for me. I'll say different things to different people. I'll just give you a part and they'll come to me for the rest." He asked me, "Do you love my people?" I said, "Yes, I love everybody." I could feel and sense His pleasure at my immediate obedience.

Little did I know we were dialoguing. (Jeremiah 1:1-10) The Word of God tells us that we know in part and we prophesy in part. I was seven when that happened. It could not have happened if my mother had not taught me to hear God at an even younger age. Years ago, she was preparing me for the call of God upon my life. Take a quick survey of your obedience to God:

What are at least five things the Lord has told you to do recently?

1._____

2._____

3._____

4._____

5._____

What are five things the Lord told you to do last year?

1._____

2._____

3._____

4._____

5._____

What are five things the Lord told you to do five years ago?

1._____

2._____

3._____

4._____

5._____

You are standing in a time where every little thing you do counts for eternity and destiny. It does not matter if you have been saved 55 days or 55 years. God is looking at this present moment and how you obey Him. The acts of obedience that you complete for Him will require inconvenience, selflessness, and courage. How do you respond to Him? We must respond to Him the same way that we want Him to respond to us.

To obey the Lord, you must rid yourself of the excuses. I have coined a name for what I believe is a major demonic spirit that causes people to miss God. I named it "The Spirit Of As Soon As I." When the Lord challenges you to do something, the automatic response of the flesh is an excuse. "As soon as I eat, as soon as I sleep, as soon as I go, as soon as I come back, as soon as I start school, as soon as I finish school, as soon as I get up, as soon as I lay down, as soon as I get married, as soon as I get divorced, as soon as I have children, as soon as the children are grown, as soon as I."

Move the "As soon as I" to the side and walk on and embrace the totality of your destiny in Christ Jesus. You have been stripped of the affordability to settle for less. You can try but it won't work. You can try to fake like you're average, you can try to be just another church, you can try to be just another Christian, but I promise you, it won't work.

On Calvary, when they stripped Christ of His dignity, He stripped you of excuses. When they stripped Him and made Him naked for all to see, He hung there publically. So there are no secrets. He said, "I'm taking this for you and I trust you to put purpose behind what I'm doing."

Now the ball is in your court. You can dribble or make a bank shot. You have two choices: to obey or disobey. You can obey and fulfill the will of God, or you can just hang around in this realm taking up space and stand in the way of those who are going on to perfection. If you obey, it will be time well spent and one of the best decisions you'll ever make. As we purpose to fulfill God's will for our lives, we encounter terrific challenge and serious struggle. Hebrews 5:8 tells us,

Though He was a Son, yet He learned obedience by the things which He suffered.

If Jesus had to suffer, what would exempt us from challenge and struggle?

When I was living in Mishawaka, Indiana, the Lord spoke to me and directed me to move to Tulsa, Oklahoma. Because I obeyed, I hit the ground running in terms of destiny. I obeyed and it caused many things to open and be made available to me.

When you are where you're supposed to be, the blessings can come overnight express instead of by wagon train! If you are going to go places in God, it will start with little acts of obedience. Most of the things God requires are not very public so flesh-governed people are not interested. People of the Spirit know that God entrusts big packages to those who are faithful with little letters. Remember that in the days to come as He approaches you with acts of obedience.

We must condition our flesh to obey God as soon as He speaks. If we are faithful over little things, promotion to greater things will follow. God is putting you into a place of supreme obedience. If you are going to go places in God, you must start with a simple "Yes Lord. I will obey you."

I was raised and rocked on the knee of the Baptist Church and for that I will always honor the Lord. I was taught that Jesus loves me. I was taught the Word of God, I was taught loyalty, respect for leadership, and submission to those over me. My mother was a Junior Matron, Sunday School teacher, and all around church worker.

Then she blew it. She had been going to prayer meetings with some holy rollers. Next thing we knew, Mama "got" the Holy Ghost. I wasn't sure if it fell on her or jumped inside her, so when she took us to the prayers meetings, I was careful to not fall asleep just in case!

I remember my mother telling us about learning to hear the voice of God and then obeying what we heard. One time, I knew Mama was cooking dinner, singing or praying in a sing-song fashion, as she always did. She rubbed her hands on her apron and rushed to the front room. She said she heard this voice tell her, "Dorothy, go stand by the green chair."

She stood by the mint chair, bowed her head, and folded her hands. She waited in total silence. Nothing happened. She asked the Lord, "Did you speak to me or am I crazy?" There was silence. She said, "Lord, you know this stuff is all new to me. I just want to make sure this is you. Is it? Did you tell me to come stand by this green chair?"

After several moments of uncomfortable silence, she turned and began the slow trek down the hall. As she left the side of the chair, that soft voice spoke again. She froze in her footsteps. This is what He said:

"Daughter, it was me speaking to you. I did tell you to stand by the green chair." She said, "But Lord I went and I did what I heard." He said, "Yes you did." And she cried, but nothing happened. He said, "You heard me *and you obeyed.*"

In that moment, God began to speak to her and tell her things little by little. As she was faithful with the little things, He began to trust her with loftier assignments. Now after over 38 years of hearing and obeying, she travels the country taking the Word of the Lord all because she stood by the green chair. I challenge you today to begin obeying the Lord when He speaks to you.

8

THE END AND THE BEGINNING

You are stripped of mediocrity. You have no entrance or accessibility into the norm for the average sweet hokey Christian. You are being challenged to stand on the very cutting edge of change and this point is razor sharp. You cannot afford to lose your balance, as something would be severed as a result.

In his book *Black Holes and Baby Universes and Other Essays*, author Stephen Hawking states "Times goes at different rates for different observers." As it is in the natural, so it is in the realm of the Spirit. Imagine two people looking at the same shooting star but from two different vantage points.

If you were perched in the window of a sixth floor Manhattan loft, your view would be limited by the skyscrapers and buildings around you. If you were in a field on a grassy knoll in the open countryside, your view would be much clearer and more beautiful.

Where you are determines what you see. That is why you must be in the right place at the right time. You can be at the right place but in the wrong time. Once you determine that you are in the right place and in the timing of God, you must extend effort and spiritual energy to see through the eyes of Christ. In the worst case scenario, Jesus saw an opportunity for a miracle. In the worst case scenario, Jesus saw an opportunity for life. You will not miss if you choose to see as Jesus did.

Einstein's theory of relativity describes how objects move through space and time. It sounds deep and heavy but it really is a spiritual principle. It shows that time is not just a universal quantity that exists on its own. We who name the Name of Christ know that time is in God and time is born of God. This is what I mean by "the vicissitudes of life." This refers to conditions of constant change as a natural process rather than an unlikely phenomenon.

Einstein maintains that the past and future are just directions in space time, similar to up and down, left and right, and day and night. Changes are going to occur as a natural part of life. Change is a part of the life force. Change is inevitable. You can resist it, you can run from it, you can try to speak it away, but change is going to occur. You can change dead or alive, but you will change. You simply must.

What is your personal or spiritual theory of relativity? How do you define the movement of your life through time and space? Is everything in your life defined by your personal experiences? Is your reality defined by things you've gone through, by your life challenges? Or is your life defined, even in the midst of change, by the unfailing Word of God? Out of everything on the planet, only the Word of God will remain.

Matthew 24:35 tells us,

Heaven and earth shall pass away but My Words shall not pass away.

Isaiah 40:8 tells us,

The grass withereth, the flower fadeth: but the Word of our God shall stand forever.

I Peter 1:25a tells us,

But the Word of Lord endureth forever. . . .

As the changes of life take you up and down, as struggles

shift from left to right, as you watch your day turn into night, the Word of God is your hope. The Word of God is the only constant in a world of variables. Things can be changed by the Word of God, but you must be changed first. The Word of God will effectively change you inside out.

In fulfilling destiny, you are only authorized to go in the future direction in time. While sitting on a beach, I watched a crab take a stroll. It was a struggle if ever I saw one. This crab looked like it was not in agreement with itself. It seemed to walk left and right at the same time, pulling its personal center askew. That is why it takes a crab so long to get anywhere. Its body is not set in agreement. It walks to the left and to the right at the same time. It eventually gets where it wants to go, it just takes much longer.

As it is in the natural, so it is in the Spirit. Your mind, will, and emotions need to come into agreement with your body and heart and all need to line up with the Word of God. Your mouth can say you are healed but if your heart does not believe it your miracle or funeral will tell the story.

You, unlike the crab, are authorized to go in one direction at a time and that is the direction that causes you to seek Jesus. You can only experience today. Yesterday is a memory. Tomorrow is a dream. Only right now is tangible. Destiny is accomplished in many different ways. You cannot and must not go back in time. That is God's job and His alone. Only He can and often when He does go back in time, it is to establish a work of healing, substantiate a premise, or redeem a moment that was outside of Him.

When you are in a Job or Jonah mode, time can feel like terror. It seems unending and slow. If you are suffering, your hearts desire is for this time to end. If you are a woman in labor pushing forth, your scream is that the time is now. Yet, if you are in a moment of ecstasy, you want the moment to last forever. You must remember that everything, good, bad, happy, or sad, has a point of origin and a point of cessation. It must have a beginning and an end. Only Father God is eternal and non-ending.

As you read this page, you have come to a crossroad. You have come to the end of this book in the natural and you have come to an end of your self in the Spirit. Now you must enter a new beginning. You cannot afford to go from this place in the same strength, with the same mind, in the same way. I believe God is dealing with you right now. I pray that you will not only hear Him but obey what you hear. This book is ending, but your new place in God is beginning. Go forward in the strength of our God and King!

The Spirit of the Lord says unto you, "Behold, I show you my finest. I cause you to behold a work of excellence wrought by mine own hand. Because I love you, I begin even now preparing you for that which is to come. And indeed, that which is to come is born of my Spirit, and it is reflected and found in thee. I now funnel into you the grace for all that lies ahead. I pour into you and I turn on full blast the spigots of my glory. I fill you up from the bottom to the top. Think it not strange that I shall use thee in the days to come.

"For you would say, 'But I am not worthy. Look not upon the mistakes of my folly.' Know ye not that I am thy Redeemer and I am accomplishing much in the midst of thee? I have spoken in times past and again I say unto thee, behold, I do a new thing. Allow me to heal your hurts, even the self-inflicted wounds. Allow me to make clean your secret places that there would be no spot found within thee.

"Bask in the wonder of my presence. Stand in awe of Who I am. For a long time have I desired this entrance into thee, and now all things are made ready. I come in and I clean. I come in and I repair. I come in and I restore. So be not afraid, for I dwell in the midst of thee to do thee good and not evil.

"The dawning of this day shall ring down the corridors of your soul because you know my voice and the movement of my flow. Consider ye not the ways of the past, for I do a new thing. Marvel not at the miracles of the past, for I do a new thing. Receive my anointing for the tasks which lie ahead. Go no more in the strength of your frailty but go clad in my armor.

"For you have entered into a season of visitation and I now visit you. Look for me on the left. Look for me on the right. Look for me in the morning. Look for me at night. For surely, I do come. I cause the winds of my Spirit to blow upon thee and bring great calm and refreshing unto thee.

"I am moving in the midst of thee and I cause thee to be still. I cause thee to be silent so that you would hear what I say unto you.

"Your greatest days are ahead and I will cause you to triumph over your every enemy. Know that I am on your side and I am moving on your behalf. Look for me, for surely I am coming to thee. Prepare thy heart, prepare thy life, prepare thy mind, prepare thy spirit or visitation is thy portion", saith the Spirit of Grace.

THE SONG OF THE LORD

In this moment and in this time
You're standing in a moment, in a moment divine
I have drawn you gently to this place
To overshadow you with my grace

All that is hath already been
And if you're not careful it will come around again
So watch and heed and hear my word
For you know me, servant, it's me you have heard

Will you take the risk
And leave the abyss
Of all that's known and familiar to you?

Will you take my hand
Will you take a stand
And allow me to move?

Will you take the risk
Will you obey
Will you stand
Or will you sway?

You've entered into a new movement of time
Time as you know time to be
If you obey, stand, and don't sway
And you'll ensure your destiny

I know your heart, I know your mind
Remember I am the Lord and I am thine
Ask what you will
But know there is a price to pay
Will you stand in the moment
Or will you sway?

Stand, Servant, Stand
Move only in me
Stand, Servant, Stand
I'll use you to set others free

Stand, Servant, Stand